Charles Wesley Bennett

History of the Philosophy of Pedagogics

Charles Wesley Bennett

History of the Philosophy of Pedagogics

ISBN/EAN: 9783744705189

Printed in Europe, USA, Canada, Australia, Japan

Cover: Foto ©Thomas Meinert / pixelio.de

More available books at **www.hansebooks.com**

HISTORY

—OF THE—

PHILOSOPHY OF PEDAGOGICS

—BY—

CHARLES WESLEY BENNETT, LL. D.

LATE PROFESSOR OF HISTORIC THEOLOGY IN
GARRETT BIBLICAL INSTITUTE

SYRACUSE, N. Y.

C. W. BARDEEN, PUBLISHER

1893

PREFACE

In the following brief sketch I have used whatever material and sources were to me available. I have not hesitated often to use the exact language of an author when this clearly expressed my meaning. If I have not, by proper marks, always indicated this my indebtedness, it will be excused in an essay of this character, laying no claim whatever to originality. I have been most indebted to the masterly treatises of von Raumer, Schmidt and Goldammer, and I desire to recommend most heartily these authors as thorough and exhaustive.

History of the Philosophy of Pedagogics

The subject is a most difficult one, as will appear from an analysis.

1. *History* means primarily "inquiry," "investigation,"—and then is applied to the *results* of this inquiry and investigation. Perhaps Cousin's definition may be good enough. "History is a complete and systematically arranged account of the successive and simultaneous developments of all the elements that constitute humanity." ["Introduction to Study of Philosophy," p. 7.]

2. *Philosophy* may be variously defined, but there is in all these diverse definitions a germinal unity. It has been called the "Science of Principles," "The explanation of the reason of things," "A collection of general laws under which all subordinate

phenomena are comprehended." "The study of universal and necessary principles considered under their different aspects, and in the great problems which they solve, is almost the whole of philosophy—it fills it, measures it, divides it." [*Cousin*, "Free, Beautiful and Good." Sect. I, p. 50.] "Philosophy is *reflection*, elevated to the rank and authority of *method*."

3. *Pedagogics* is the science and art of so developing, by means of *conscious influence* on the physical, intellectual, and moral powers of man, the ideas of truth, freedom, and love that lie at the foundation of his god-derived nature, that he can meet spontaneously, and independently, his human responsibilities." (*Schmidt*, "Gesch. d. Erziehung," p. 1.)

We are, then, assigned the following task —"to give a complete and systematically arranged account of the general and necessary principles and laws by which there has been developed, by a conscious influence on the physical, intellectual and moral powers of the unfolding man, those ideas of truth, freedom and love that lie at the foundation of his god-derived nature, so that he can spontaneously and independently meet human responsibilities."

You will immediately perceive that the field is too vast even for the most cursory examination within the time allotted to us. I have, after considerable reflection, concluded to pass by the history of the nations of antiquity, to omit all examination of the educational theories of the Christian Fathers in the Romish and Byzantine Churches, as well as the struggles of mediæval times, marvellous as they were, and briefly touch upon some of the most important and influential systems that have appeared in the Post-Reformation period.

I. THE REFORMERS AS EDUCATORS

A revolution in thought and life so radical and far-reaching as that of the Reformation of the 16th Century, could not leave the great subject of educational methods unexamined. The contrasts between the mediæval or church spirit, and the spirit of the new era, were sharp and irreconcilable.

1. It was the subjective *vs.* the objective.

2. It was the life of man in God and the life

of God in man as the original revelation, *vs.*
the binding power of external authority.

3. It was the fullest freedom of faith and
knowledge, *vs.* traditional creeds.

4. It was the authority of conscience, *vs.*
the authority of the Church or anything
else whatsoever.

Justin's principle was accepted by the
new era—" Christ is the eternal reason, with
which the whole human race may become
participant, and they are Christians who
live according to this eternal reason." Protestantism saw that the schools were the
training places for the callings of life—so
that not *one* class or calling—whether ruler,
or clergy, or knight—but *all* alike should
here be prepared for life's duties. The in-
violability of the individual carried with it
the duty of arousing the people to a sense of
their responsibility to God and the State.

So the contrast of the Pre-Reformation
school idea to the Reform idea is sharp.
The mediæval and Catholic idea was that
education must be *special*—the Latin schools
to educate the clergy and government officials—the schools of arithmetic and writ-
ing for business men—the girls' schools to

educate the wives, etc., etc. The peculiar
product and property of Protestantism was
education for *man* AS *man*—as a creature
endowed with power and awful responsibility. " The primary school of the Reformers
was based on the idea that each one was to
be his own priest, and that each was to *per-
fect in himself* this salvation to which he
was called ; and, therefore, that each should
walk in *immediate* relation to God and the
truth.

The translation of the Bible into the vernacular and its wide diffusion, worked won-
ders among the people in Germany and
England.   Erasmus, Luther, Melanchthon,

ERASMUS.

Calvin, Zwinglius
and all the reform-
ers had a keen ap-
preciation of the
duty of care for
the young. Luth-
er regarded this
as the noblest
work in which
man could engage,
and thought that
Christianity could be powerful only as it

scrupulously provides for the education of the children. His theory is—" God sustains the church through the schools—they are the *fountains*—the *seed* of the church." " And just as government compels the subjects in case of war to bear the sword or knapsack, so much more ought it to *compel* subjects to educate their children." In the order of excellence of subjects Luther ranks *religion* first and uppermost—next he esteems *language* most valuable. With language the exact sciences are not to be neglected. He ranks history very high— logic is less prized, since it gives no new capacity, as he thought. Rhetoric, gymnastics, and music were invaluable.

The high promises of the Reformers were not however to be realized. The fatal error they committed was in attempting to make the schools aids to advance their peculiar religious tenets, and in regarding instruction in Christianity as the chief end and duty of the schools. They knew not how to tolerate purely secular learning. The spirit of the reformation was well nigh quenched in a war of dogmatic formulas, and by the mutual hate and jealousy of par-

ties whose real interest was mainly in a set-
tled harmony. Scholasticism again revived,
and we have the second stage,—that of abstract theological education.

II. ABSTRACT THEOLOGICAL EDUCATION

This reached from the middle of the 16th
to the 18th Century. This period is marked
by the prominence of theologic and philosophic studies to the exclusion of what are called
natural sciences. If the latter were at all
introduced it was more for *practical utility*
than *scientific value.* Education and instruction under this plan consisted largely
in loading the memory with mere formulas.
No opportunity was given for the free exercise of the powers of reason and imagina-
tion in any direction that was pleasing, and
in modes most natural to the individual.

Melanchthon's celebrated "Saxon School
Plan," that played so important a part in
Germany and in other European countries,
proposed : 1. To assemble the pupils morn-
ing and evening in the church, for hearing
the Bible and prayers ; at the evening service Latin hymns were to be chanted. 2.
The Latin language was to be cultivated to

the neglect of the vernacular. 3. The master was not to be so much a helper of the pupils as an object of their *reverence*. 4. The *religious* (really the sectarian element) was to predominate in the instruction of all the various classes

MELANCHTHON.

into which he divided the pupils. 5. The *memory* was to be crowded with the formulas of the church, and with sentences prepared by the teacher.

The same order, in all essentials, was followed by Bugenhagen in his "Church order for Brunswick"—placing all under the oversight of the officials and clergy. Also, this was closely imitated in Wittenberg. Religion and Latin were the chief subjects of instruction. The higher differed from the lower in that the higher had reference to the preparation for clerical orders, and introduced logic and rhetoric, and a little more freedom was allowed to students for self-government and independent study. While the celebrated William Wolf uttered a protest against this system in declaring that *thought, not religious hair-splitting,* was a preparation for a pure life ; and love to God and man, *not* the inculcation of bigoted dogmas —the chief object of education; and Trotzendorf and Sturm claimed that teaching was a *high art* that needed most careful study for its successful

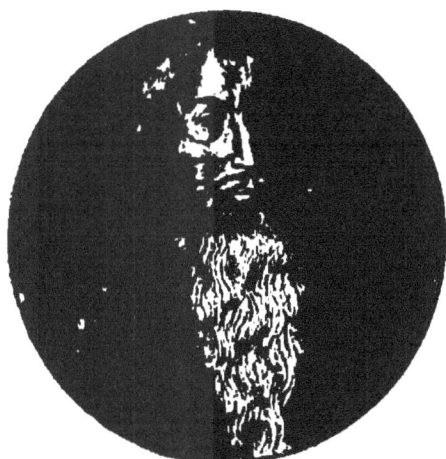

STURM.

practice, the religious and political strifes of the Protestants worked the death of good instruction and tended to foster the spirit and modes of the Scholastic Philosophy, and to dwarf the powers by a discussion of the most minute and barren technicalities. The school was a place of dread and gloom to the pupils—the veriest "vale of tears" to the youth of this unfortunate period.

III. A HOPEFUL REVOLT

It was to be expected that there would come a serious revolt against a system so unnatural and barren of results. It came from several sources, and worked a new and hopeful condition of things. The sources of this opposition may be summed thus :

1. Inside the Romish Church, *Jesuitism* represented reformation of educational methods as well as opposition to Protestantism.

2. *Jansenism* represented a still more radical reformation in education, as in religion, within the Catholic Church.

3. *Pietism* represented the protest in the Protestant Church against the dead, dry, educational methods, as well as against a drear religious formalism.

4. More powerful than all, perhaps, was the revolt of Philosophy in the Empiricism of Locke, and the Inductive system of Bacon.

1. Jesuitism

opposed the freedom of the Reformation with its own freedom, which consists in the denial of all freedom to the man ; hence in the denial of human nature, in the denial

of morality, and of Christianity itself.   It
appealed to the ambition and avarice of
men.   With a sharp and vigorous mind, it
followed out its policy.   It used men of
gifted natures to inculcate its doctrine that
mankind, like a wild beast, must be tamed,
in order to be ruled.

But its outward methods were almost the
opposite of the Protestant.   It substituted
mildness, ease and grace of manner, and pol-
ish for harshness, severity and solidity of
attainments.   Latin and poetry were the
chief studies.   To speak Latin and not the
vernacular was peremptory.   Classical studies were only useful, however, to improve
the *style,* and not, as in Protestantism, a
mere servant of theology.   Mathematics,
geography, the vernacular, and even music,
were neglected.

Obedience to superiors, was the central
idea of the system.   *Emulation* was among
the chief motives.   Prizes, rewards, dis-
tinctions, all appealing to this principle,
were a large part of the machinery of this
order.   Corporal punishment was discoun-
tenanced, and seldom practised.   The high-
est duty of the teacher was thoroughly to

know his pupils. To change natural affection into affection for the order, was a constant aim of effort.

The instruction of the Jesuits was very mechanical—leaving small and meager opportunity for the exercise of the powers of reason. They cared little for primary schools except so far as they might find among the masses those who might give rich promise of aid and honor to the Order.

2. *Jansenism*

Not less strong, and vastly more salutary, was the opposition to the dead scholastic orthodoxy of Protestantism and the pretensions of the Romish Hierarchy that came from Pietism and Jansenism. In many things they were closely related. They represent a true spiritual and religious feeling that desired to break through the constraints of form, and reach the central essence of Christianity. The Jansenists in Holland and France, the Puritans and Methodists in England and Scotland, and the Pictists in Germany and Switzerland, were powerful in breaking through the dead methods of abstract theologic, as well as the hierarchic systems of education, and infusing a new vigor into this most important department of labor.

With its errors, Jansenism, nevertheless, manifested a most glowing love for the young—an unselfish surrender of itself to the interests of education and the race. In matters of instruction it developed a method simple, rational, and adapted to nature. It inculcated the union of a more fundamental study of religion with thorough mastery of language and philosophy. Port Royal furnished the most thoroughly prepared and philosophical text-books of that age. Even after the suppression of Port Royal and the scattering of the Jansenists, its spirit was perpetuated in Fenelon and Rollin, and reached into high places through the matchless eloquence of the Court Preacher. [See his "*de l' Education des filles*," dedicated to the Duchess of Beauvilliers.]

In England we hear the earnest protest of the Puritans in the 17th, and of the Methodists in the 18th century, against the formalism in religion and the pedagogical methods of the established church. Milton had roused the kingdom by his trumpet tones, sounding a better method in education; the Methodists had shamed the slothfulness of the establishment by furnishing religious instruction to the masses, and gathering the neglected children into Sunday schools. In his work on education Milton had advocated an equal attention to language and to the sciences. He gave a plan of instruction far richer in spirit and extent than had hitherto been known—arguing for a *general* culture to the exclusion of *professional* studies.

3. Pietism

Even more powerful for reform in religion and in educational methods were the Pietists of Germany. Philip Jacob Spener, of whom it has been said "the world was not worthy," Count Zinzendorf, and, most of all, Augustus Hermann Franke, in Halle, brought in a better day for the science of Pedagogics. Pietism sent a new vigor through the entire school life of Europe. It gave rise to better methods; it created normal schools; it furnished for Germany vastly improved text-books; it brought the

schools back from the cloister to every-day
life; it was the first to conceive of the
schools as an organic whole, resting at last
upon primary education.

The ground principle of Pietism was,—
without genuine piety all knowledge, all
worldly wisdom, all culture are more hurt-
ful than useful. Piety comports with every
lawful position and calling in life. First,
and foremost, therefore, must education
strive after and guard itself by a radical
improvement of the *heart*.

The law of the educational method of
Pietism was a continuous *conversation* with
the pupils. *Catechism* is the very *soul* of
instruction. Thus is learning made lighter,
the intercourse of teacher and pupil becomes
intimate. Yet this catechetical instruction
must be conducted so carefully and skilfully
as to strengthen and not to weaken the intellectual powers. The education of the
memory was careful, the understanding was
vigorously exercised, and the *pen* was freely
used with a view to exactness of expression.

We cannot too highly estimate the bene-
ficial work of Pietism in the pedagogical

methods of Continental Europe. The effects
reach to our own day.

4. The Realistic-Philosophic Opposition to Scholasticism and to the Romish Hierarchy

It is time to turn to another source of
opposition to Scholasticism in Pedagogics
and to the methods of the Roman Hierachy.
It came from the side of Philosophy. The
instruction had become dead and formal—
it yielded no rich and generous fruit. Books,
mere books, words, terms—with no breath
of life in them. Terms and not things,—
*words about things,—not the things them-
selves.* Princi-
ples were scarce-
ly thought of.

Montaigne
(1533–1592), in
France, and *Ba-
con* (1561–1626,)
in England, suc-
ceeded by *Locke*
(1632–1704),
were the great

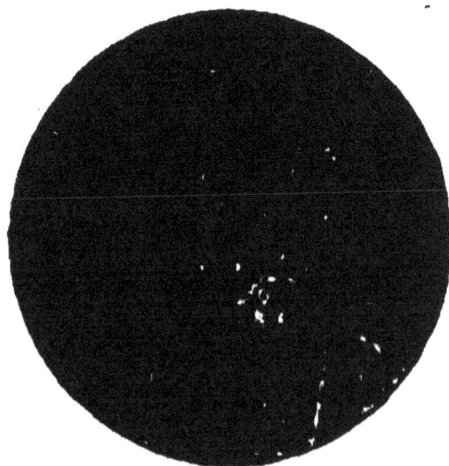

MONTAIGNE.

revolutionists to overturn the scholastic

methods.   Montaigne, so early as the middle of the 16th century, had become disgusted with the fruitlessness of the prevailing systems.   He said—"We may take meat into the stomach as long as we please, and it will be all in vain unless it is digested and become a part of ourselves—incorporated into our system."   Pedagogues and reformers should not speak as from a *book*, but from their *own thought*—from an *opinion* intelligently formed by their own *investigation*.   This that now seems a truism in pedagogical science, was with Montaigne's contemporaries scarcely thought of.   He regarded the vernacular of more importance than the dead languages, or any foreign language. This was a revolution, indeed.

Bacon, the reviver, illustrator, and defender of *Realism*, in his "Inductive Philosophy," by inviting the mind to leave the dead past, to contemplate the living present, and to look into living nature with open eyes, lays the very foundation of realistic educational methods.

He thus became the real father of all Trade-Schools, of Polytechnic Schools, etc., etc.

Locke, by looking into mind itself—by studying anew its nature, its laws and its processes, bases afterwards in his "Thoughts on the education of Children," his entire pedagogical views upon his philosophy. "A sound mind in a sound body," is the foundation axiom of his whole system. Keep the body sound—treat children as *reasonable beings, not as things*—preserve their individuality—check their selfishness—inculcate self-government—let the restraint come from *within*, through a cultivation of the conscience and will—*not* from *without*, by means of rods and fear.

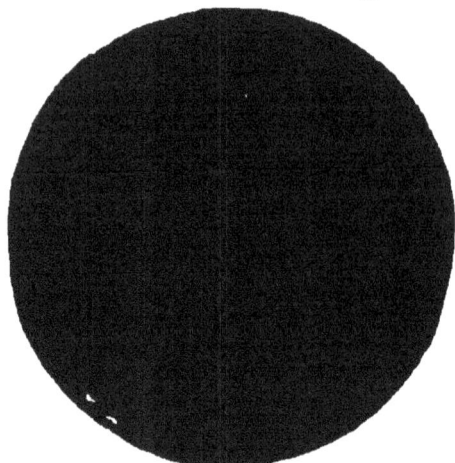

LOCKE.

Praise and blame are healthful motives—corporal punishment is an extreme measure. Let praise be given in the presence of others, that it may not only stimulate the recipient, but his fellows as well—administer reproof and blame to the child alone, lest he may lose his self-respect, as well as become a mark

for the ridicule of his associates.   A ground
or reason for his discipline must ever exist
in the mind of the teacher, and this should,.
as far as possible, be made known to the
pupil—specially by means of examples drawn
from history or from analagous cases sup-
posed.

Through the entire course of the child's.
training the desire for knowledge must be
fostered.   Inquiring children must be en-
couraged, not chilled by rebuke or neglect.
Play must be allowed—work must be made to
seem a recreation, not a task.   Mere assigned
tasks are not recommended.   No help should
be furnished by the teacher when there is.
self-help.   The child should learn to read
as soon as he learns to talk, and a foreign
language must be learned as we learn our
mother tongue.   Latin is early recommended.   Yet the vernacular was far better than
all other languages.

Locke's theory of education is strictly *util-
itarian*.   A well-trained, well-appointed man
of the world was the product.

In Germany the anti-scholastic methods,
from a philosophical stand-point, received
marked attention, and were wonderfully

forwarded by such masters of pedagogics as *Wolfgang Ratichius* (1571-1635), *John Amos Comenius,* and others.

Ratichius exclaims, " Antiquity is *played out*—reason is now victorious." His principles were clearly conceived and thoroughly wrought out. They were reduced to a few heads as follows :

1. Everything according to the order and course of nature.

2. One thing at a time, one study at a time, one author only from which to learn a language.

3. One thing oft repeated and deeply impressed.

4. The vernacular first and foremost.

5. No constraint, since this is unnatural.

6. No more memorizing,—since anything repeated to the understanding will necessarily be seized and retained by the memory. Hence lectures were repeated often, and no questions were asked during the progress of the lecture, lest the impression might be impaired by this interruption.

7. Uniformity in everything,—ever pursuing the same method in all stages of edu-

cation, and in all things pertaining to the same stage.

8. First the *thing*—then the *mode* of the thing,—first the *materials and principles*, then the *rules*.

9. Everthing through experience, therefore no authority without a reason.

Ratichius's system resulted in *practical* failure, since it degenerated into foolish extremes, that defeated the very end he himself had proposed.

Comenius had great preference for the

COMENIUS.

Sciences. His plan was to represent every-thing possible to the senses. Seeing is demonstration and believing — what we know must be learned. What is learned must be treated as present, and estimated according to its *uses*. What is learned must be learned *directly*, not in a round-about-way, —it must be learned as it is—*i. e.*, according to its *causes* or *origin ;*—the parts of a subject must be understood according to their order, position and connection.

Everything, therefore, by a natural succession,—studying one thing at a time. A subject must be continued until thoroughly mastered. Differences in pupils must be noted in order that modes may be adapted to each. All knowledge should go towards the *elevation* of the man : indeed, *morality* is vastly more than *erudition*.

A school without discipline is like a mill without water. This discipline, however, should have more reference to the characters of the pupils than to the studies themselves. Yet discipline should not prostrate and discourage, but elevate and advance the pupil. A high sense of honor and duty must be awakened, that will lead to a free-will service. With some curious and untenable notions, Comenius's system was complete, very thoroughly thought out,—expressing sound views of human nature and of the duties and methods of education, and its influence was very widely extended, and very lasting in its effects.

IV. HUMANISM

But it was not to be expected that the realistic school would proceed unquestioned and unchallenged as to its methods. Indeed, this extreme would provoke the opposite,— as has ever been true in the history of human development. So that during the 18th century there is noticed a growing spirit of criticism of the pedagogical theories of realism, as well as of the partial and excessive religious discipline of the Pietists. It gave rise to the *humanistic school*, that taught that the goal and purpose of all education is to cultivate a purely human sentiment, and to awaken in the *individual*, the *idea of humanity*.

The sole means necessary to this end, according to this school, was a thorough study of classical antiquity, its language, its laws, its antiquities. The ancient languages were the sole foundation of all true culture. Greek and Latin literature are the sources of all true and genuine erudition,—and contain accounts of all religions. The Roman jurisprudence embodies the spirit and essence of all that is truly valuable in law. The fundamentals of medicine are here found,—and

philosophy, rhetoric, logic, poetry and history,—all that is valuable or necessary—are
discussed in these ancient classical writings.

Therefore, this theory of education con-
fined the student in all the preparatory
schools to the study of language,—leaving
what are technically called *sciences* exclu-
sively to the University. It found its most
zealous advocates in Germany, though it
was widespread in its influence, and has
largely affected the college curriculum of
England and America. It gave Germany
the leadership in Classical Erudition—a
leadership that she has maintained to the
present hour. Such men as Cellarius, Gesner,
Ernesti, Heyne, Boeckh, etc., etc., are the
direct product of this school, or its most
successful advocates.

V. DEISM

It is high time that we turn our thoughts
to a most remarkable educational phenom-
enon that appeared in England, France and
Germany. It was the other extreme of a
perverted Pietism, and the artificial, stilted,
social forms that had been imposed on
France by Louis XIV., and had found their
way into England through the Restoration.

This is usually known under the term *Deism.* The kernel thought of this system is that nothing can be certain to man that is not in accordance with the laws of his understanding,—that self-consciousness is the acme and ultimate for man,—that revelation, as it is called, may be useful to educate the crude masses, but is not necessary to Philosophy. It, therefore, rejects all that is supernatural in the Christian religion, and retains only what is common to all religions.

The principles that are claimed to be thus common to all religions are as follows :

1. There is one Supreme God.

2. This Supreme God ought to be worshiped.

3. Virtue and Piety are the most essential requisites to this Divine reverence and worship.

4. Man is under obligations to repent of and forsake his sins.

5. Good and Evil will be rewarded in this life and the life to come.

, All beyond these five principles was regarded superfluous, and the invention of an ambitious priesthood.

The work that most completely embodies these principles in a system of education, is

Defoe's "Robinson Crusoe." It really incorporates into itself the ground principles of Deism : unfolding under its pleasing narrative a theory of human development by mere natural processes. It is the picture of a child of nature overcoming obstacles, and being educated by these struggles with nature independently of the artificial helps of society. We all know what a marvellous popularity this work immediately enjoyed. Its translation into all the languages of Europe disseminated its doctrines throughout the entire continent, and awakened an intense enthusiasm in many of the master thinkers of the 18th century.

The man who embraced its principles most completely, and pushed them to a last extreme, was *Rousseau*, in his celebrated work —"Emile." This work reveals the thought of this wonderful man with regard to what he regards

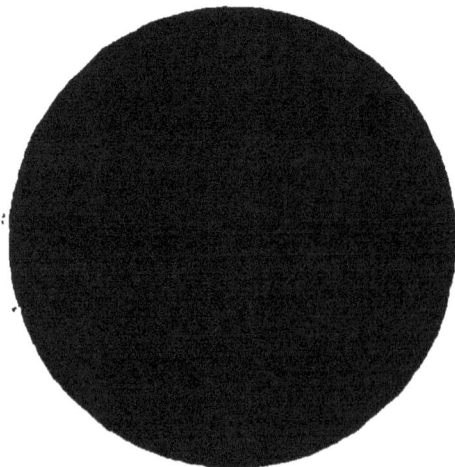

ROUSSEAU.

the true theory of education. The whole theory is—Society is a *curse*—a state of abject *bondage*, that must be broken. He would have the child put forth its activities under no constraint,—let the child strive to gain something because it needs it,—let its *instincts* guide it to just what its nature craves. Obedience is not a motive or an end —*necessity* of the nature is the law. The words "obedience" and "command" he would blot out of the lexicons.

He would not have a child see a book before he is twelve years of age. The earliest education needs only to be *negative*—it does not consist in distinguishing virtue from vice, but in guarding the heart from mistakes, and the intellect from errors. His dogma is that all evil is the result of circumstances; these circumstances being largely products and concomitants of society and government. Hence the correction for these evils is a return to a state of nature,—breaking through all artificial shackles that now bind us.

We see at a glance that Rousseau had by no means solved the deep problem of education,—since he had recognized man neither

as a member of society nor in the enjoyment
of all his powers. So that his so-called
natural development becomes, in fact, the
most *unnatural.* Yet the effect of his treat-
ise was powerful and far-reaching. It continued its influe-
ence for nearly a
half century in
France and Ger-
many. It was the
immediate fore-
runner and induc-
ing cause of the
efforts of Basedow
in Germany, that
resulted in t h e

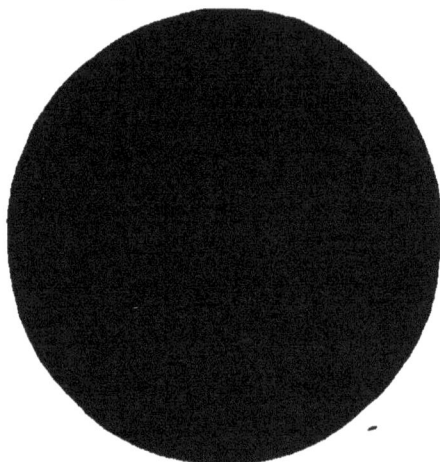

BASEDOW.

founding of his celebrated " Philanthrop-
inum," and in the wide diffusion of a theory
of Pedagogy that worked most disastrous
results on German social life and patriotism.
The energies of this noble people had been
completely sapped by the sickly sentimental-
ism that sprung from *Philanthropinism,* so
that when the proud and victorious Napoleon
marched on Berlin, he made the Prussian
capital an easy prey.

We have not the time to trace the wonder-

ful transition in the Educational method of
Germany effected through the noble labors
of Fichte and Schleiermacher, by which the
moral element was reinstated and patriotism
reinvigorated, so that from the plains of
Leipzig the proud invader was hurled across
the Rhine and sent a prisoner to Elba. It
is a chapter in the History of the Philosophy
of Pedagogics full of instruction and full of
solemn warning to our own land.

VI. FREEDOM OF ACTIVITY

We have only time to mention the last
stage of this History, viz., that in which the
free, untrammeled, activity of the human
intellect in every department of research
and discovery has been associated with a
more profound sense of religious need ; in
which the enterprise of commerce, the
facility of national intercourse, the conquests
over nature, the sacredness of individual
rights, have all united to realize a better,
purer type of civilization than the world has
before seen.

The great genius of this last era of Educational Philosophy is emphatically *Pestalozzi*. His personal history and his methods have been made so familiar to us through Mr. Barnard's work " Pestalozzi and

PESTALOZZI.

Pestalozzianism," that we need spend little time on this sketch. Dr. Karl Schmidt has said of him :

" Unattractive in outer appearance, poorly clad, often unwashed, with matted hair, with shoes run down at the heels, and with stockings often half covering them,—lacking in calm discretion,—with little tact in business,—without social shrewdness,—through his all-embracing love, through his readiness to sacrifice in helping the distressed and down-trodden, and which could send him to cut off his silver shoe-buckles for a beggar and then bind on his shoes with straw, he has, through his humility, his modesty, his unselfishness, wherein none of his contemporaries approached him,—harmless, and yielding as a child,—mild and teachable, tender and full of feeling,—inspired the world with the duty of ennobling the race, and in the long-continued contest against the coarse or more refined Materialism of his age, against the narrow Egoism and the trivial and painful Utilitarianism of the period, has lifted high the abiding ideal of human life, and labored for the good of the race and for the natural development of the mind of the child."

The ground philosophical principle of this whole system is—" Proceed from intuition to notion." This does not imply however, a mere *passive receptivity*, but a *spontaneous, active receiving*. As soon as the senses receive their first impressions, begins the development of the powers of the man. The means used by him are to place the education of the people under the *mother's* care, and erect the *home* into a school.

This idea he actualized by giving to mothers a Book on Education—" The Book for Mothers," the first of the kind, it is believed, that had ever appeared. If the home is not a holy temple of God, if the mother

fails to vivify and inspire the heart and mind
of the child then all thorough reform of
the social condition is impossible.

This is the fundamental note that rings
through all his works.   Already at the cradle
of the unreasoning child, must we begin to
snatch the race from blinding deceiving in-
fluences, and place it in the hands of a better
power which the experience of the centuries
has enabled us to deduce in relation to
mental and moral laws.   This need of ele-
mentary work is general.   The mother in her
processes must follow the course agreeable
to the nature of the child,—so also must the
school.   All school cultivation that does not
thus accord must lead astray.   Humanity is
like in its nature, its needs and its goal ;
hence a like discipline is demanded for all
and evermore.

Such in imperfect outline is the Philosophy of Education of Pestalozzi.

In this connection one more man must be
mentioned, whose zeal and success in primary
instruction entitle him to a high place among

FRŒBEL

original workers in the Philosophy of Education. I refer of course to Frœbel—the real founder of t h e *Kindergarten* in Germany. He agreed entirely with Pestalozzi in his high estimate of family training—going so far as to assert that so long as the mother neglects to train her child according to the laws of its nature, all attempted reforms in the schools will be in vain.

His observation that the first dawnings of child-life were accompanied with desires for activity and motion led him to the determination of the laws of this activity, and to the devising of means of conserving this restlessness to useful and educating ends. Since activity is the very condition of development, to guide this activity into right channels he regarded all important. Noticing what was universal—that is, the *law* of the action of the child—he reached this result—" that the nature of the child manifests itself *universally in play.* No more true is it that birds build nests, or foxes dig holes, or bees form cells, than that children play ;—*it is their nature.*"

Therefore, to develop and educate the young mind by means of play, is the central idea of Frœbel's system.

We cannot pursue the system further. Suffice it to say that these two,—Pestalozzi and Frœbel—are the *coryphei* of modern primary instruction,—exerting an influen ce this hour on modern civilization that is entirely inconceivable.

The fulness of this sketch might lead me to touch upon the more modern developments in the science of Pedagogy—and speak of the modifying force of certain dogmas of modern philosophic thought—such as Comte and his school—Herbert Spencer, J. Stuart Mill, Hamilton, etc., etc. I deem it best not to trespass upon the territory of these essayists.

CONCLUSION

The History of the Philosophy of Pedagogics has proved to me a most interesting and instructive study. It seems to me that

no one who makes any considerable preten-
sion to thoroughness as an Educator, can
afford to neglect it. It certainly shows us
that Pedagogics is no chance work that
every *dabbler* or *pedant* is well able to under-
take, but rather the most serious, difficult
and far-reaching in its consequences to the
individual, the family, and the State. It
teaches us that those great. thinkers that
tower like Alps above their fellows, have regarded its study with the profoundest interest, and have brought to the solution of
its hard problems their choicest powers.

It likewise teaches us that there *is* a deep
Philosophy of Pedagogics—a Philosophy that
has to do with subjects of no less interest
than the *nature* of man, the *destiny* of man,
and the *means* by which this nature can
realize this destiny. At a glance we see that
the Philosophy of Pedagogics is only a branch
or corollary of General Philosophy ; that it
ever has shifted, and ever will shift, with a
shifting Psychology, with a shifting Theology, with a shifting Philosophy of History,
and with the shifting views of the doctrine
of final causes. If man is of the Earth,
earthy—after a few days of struggling and

of tears to return to dust to rise no more ;—
if History at best is only *your* incoming on
the stage to mount on the shoulders of your
predecessors, and *my* incoming to mount on
yours ;—you and I alike serving our brief
purpose, yet to have no share in some final
triumph,—then the Philosophy of Pedagogics is *one* thing,—it *may* have its motives ;
we *may*, possibly, find our inspiration to
work.

But if the History of Education is like
Universal History—a History of Mankind
" *by* God *through* God, *to* God,"—if Christ
is the middle point of Universal History,
also of the History of Pedagogics, if my
sacrifice is to contribute to the elevation not
of my immediate successor alone, but to the
final triumph, which I, too, am to share ;—
if my destiny is bound up intimately with
the destinies of the race, and the destinies
of the race are affected by my conduct ; if,
in short, this historic drama is the necessary
medium of moral development to the race,
which shall clearly appear in the grand *de-
nouement ;*—then this work of ours *has* its
motives,—it *has* its inspiration,—*I* know it,
—*you* feel it,—and we are willing, fellow

workers, to toil on in obscurity, if needs be, —little appreciated it may be,—poorly requited often,—but still proud, and satisfied, because co-workers with the Great Teacher in lifting the race from bondage to freedom, and from darkness to the light of life.

www.ingramcontent.com/pod-product-compliance
Lightning Source LLC
Chambersburg PA
CBHW032138080426
42733CB00008B/1116